The Heart, the Home and the Fog

Kimberley Graham

BookLeaf Publishing
India | USA | UK

Presentation by *BookLeaf Publishing*

Web: www.bookleafpub.com

E-mail: info@bookleafpub.com

ISBN: 978-93-5744-932-8

First edition 2022

To all those who inspire me, and anyone who
has ever made it through the fog.

PREFACE

I hope these poems make you smile.

Believe in magic

When a child believes in magic
They can look beyond the tragic
They see the beauty in the world
And their dreams will be impearled

They will see shapes in the clouds
Admire the shadows in crowds
They'll tell stories of imps in the hedges
Fairies on ledges
And friendly ghosts in the edges

When their imagination gets fed
Their education will be led
For they will be well read
And never short of bread

Big dreams make big plans
That use many hands
That shape the lands
From whence they came

When dreamers take action
There will be no bad traction
For that is the attraction

Teach a child to believe

With hard work and pure heart
And they will save the world

Home

What makes a house a home
And halts the call to roam
Is it hidden in the chromosome?
Or do we breathe it in the air?
What is it that makes us care?
How do you make the change
I find it all quite strange
To make the big exchange
From unplanned gypsie
Getting tipsy

To one who pays the bills
Waits patiently at tills
And picks up random spills
Who does cooking with ingredients
Without an ounce of disobedience

Brings bags to shops
And never drops
The produce on the floor
Calling everyone a whore
Unable to carry more

What makes a person sleep
Without the need to weep
At nine pm at night

It gives me quite a fright
Outside is still quite bright

To me it felt like giving up
But then I got a pup
And when his big brown eyes
Look deep through my disguise
I know that time just flies

I know his life in earth
Will bring every one much mirth
I am happy for his birth
And nothing is much sweeter
Than curling by the heater

His time is far too short
And I will stay here in our fort
Wandering why I had resisted
I knew not that life consisted
Of a love that could be gifted

My dog is a soul of gold
If truth be told
I am completely sold
On a life on the sofa
With you growing old

My son

You will never know
How I love to watch you grow
How I long for snow
Just so we can slow

But I fear as you get older
I don't want you to grow colder
And sit alone and smoulder

I just want to hug you close
And ensure your loved the most
Take walks along the coast
And look out for the pirate ghost

I want you to thrive
And learn how to drive
To really feel alive
And accomplish all you strive

I wish you true happiness
I'm not good at all this sappiness
I want to chase away the crappiness

But when I am gone
Please remember these words

When you see the trees
Think of the roots that we planted
When you see rocks
Think of the stones that we painted
When you see the ocean
Think of splashes in time
When you see clouds
Think of far away dragons

When you take a deep breath
Think of my love for you
Think always of the golden rule
Know my love is true
You are my baby
Forever and always.

I still believe

I still believe
That good will arrive
I still believe
That we will survive
That someone,
Somewhere cares
I believe in the
kindness of strangers
The avoidance of dangers
In random acts warming the heart
And that spontaneous joy
can start
Future adventures
That are retold by a fire
In times most dire
I still believe in love
I still believe in friendships
I believe in family
Be they blood born
Or forged in tears
I still have faith in the world
And in you,
Even if we've never met

I am here

The window stands ajar
The curtains have been spread
And the sunlight's seeping in

Why do you lurk
In the shadows of the room

Gentle breeze comes wisping in
A cat rests by your hand
A soft reminder of kinder times

Why do you lurk
In the shadows of the room

The candle is burning
Barely a smile to be seen
While the flame jumps playfully
just for you

Why do you lurk
In the corners of the room

Laughter fills the air
A comrade calls your name
To come towards to the light

Why do you lurk
In the shadows of the room

Do you see a darkness
That no others can view
Can you feel the cold
While the sun blazes down

Is your vision full of fog
Do you fear the noises
The unwanted touches
The paralysing stares
and the false promises

Why do you lurk
In the shadows of the room

Come out my friend and play
Come out my friend and shout
Come out my friend and battle
Battle fears and battle foes

Search for strength
Reach out for Hope
Come out my friend
Just one step for now

Come out my friend
For I am waiting

Not with malice
Not with hurt

I am waiting with your army
I am part of your great team
There are those that know your troubles
And those that don't

Some of us have demons
And some of us have answers
I am here my friend
With outstretched hand

Just one more step
For I am here

I knew not

There had been a parasite
Laying dormant in my heart
And in my soul.
While it slept
It used my hope to thrive
I knew not of its existence
I knew not why
my heart had ached
And why the world
was so much
darker Than before

I knew not of my disability
My inability to love,
To dream,
To see the paths before me.

Then one day you materialised
Before my weary eyes
And I felt a creature stir
It rose a fear in me
I thought perhaps the darkness
That had at once consumed me
Was maybe just the start.

That this new life form
Was being born into existence
To lead me further down
The perilous and foggy road.

I feared far worse than
The hell where I had been
I knew not that the kiss
that we had shared
Removed the parasite
Removed the worm
Removed the reason I was lost

You woke me up
Not in some dramatic fashion
No flamboyant gesture
No words of love
Or act of lust

Just a kiss
So full of potential
So full of all the hope
that I had seeped
So gentle and yet so strong
The sparks shone bright
And only three words spoken
But uttered with a smile
That cast away the burdens.

'That was nice' was sang
But unspoken and much louder
The souls they roared,
'At last we are complete
At last we are both free'

I knew not that my release
Had been so close, so long.
I knew not that you were the key to me,
And I the key to you
I knew not but I know now

Let's see what next we shall unlock.

The solitary magpie

The solitary magpie
Makes the military sigh
He is legendary
And he is necessary
The sight of him can horrify
And purify the guilty

He commands respect
You must salute or he'll dissect
His uniform is black and white
And he can cause a blight
So endure that you have checked

Say hello and sing the rhyme
Be sure it's in good time
Don't make him stare you down
For he is certainly no clown
And he is always in his prime

Alone he stands for sadness
Driving viewers to a madness
But when he is in love
And flies in happiness above
Two magpies bring much gladness

So when you see

Him in a tree
He may not bring bad tiding
His lover may be hiding
Look closer before you flee

There's more to magpies with every blink

Phone a friend

A minute before the metal made a mark
Her movements lost momentum
Just one moment had changed the Course
Not just of the blade,
Not just of her life
But of every soul She encountered thereafter
One pause,
One delay,
One answered call
That one distraction changed everything
That's the power of a friend
Who truly intends
And doesn't pretend
To care for you fully
So pick up the phone
Ensure no one is alone

The end

When those you love just take
You feel an unbearable ache
You question if all was fake
It's time for the inevitable break

It's hard to walk away
Even when the memories are grey
What have you got to say
Who was the hunter and who was prey

We share many tales
Explored many trails
And comforted through numerous fails
navigated dangerous gales

I can see where this path takes us
And I'm waiting for the bus
I've pushed out all the puss
There's no need for any fuss

Sometimes things were good
Other times were viewed through a hood
I could never handle your mood
I hope this won't cause a freud

But it's come time to leave
And though we may grieve
We must use our own sleeve
And choose not to deceive
There's much more we can both achieve

Symbiosis

The mountains loom high
As though they are trying to breach the sky
And explore the stars far above
They persevere and fight against
The force of gravity
And though they may crumble
They grow ever stronger.
For every stone that falls,
It strengthens its foundations
Making it more resilient
And capable of more.

The river is the only thing
That makes a continuous mark
Upon its stoney face
But it does so slowly and gently
It does not feel the need
To show obscene feats of strength
And so
The mountain does not retaliate
The river has won
before the mountain
Even knew there was a duel

Their symbiosis
Their partnership

By neithers conscious design
Has created an environment
That breathes life into many ecosystems

The water feeds the grass
That feeds the livestock
That feed the humans
That climb the mountain
And try in their own way
To beat the forces that push them down.

We are all symbiotic
We are all particles
We are all capable

Frozen

I could be a frozen swan
Or a frozen drake
I could be a cold goose
Or a sun craved owl

I could be anything
So long as it were ice
I chose these creatures
As I long for flight

I desire adventure
And smiles without forethought
To cast my arms out
And twirl in a meadow

Without fear of a blow
Caused by an involuntary pout
That had been cunningly caught
I must learn to be a shadow

During hours of the light
I shall be taught by teachers
In rooms filled with mice
And my arm in a sling

I feel like throwing in the towel

And tying up the noose
I'm so tired of doing nought but shake
I'm ready to be gone

But then I see a sign
A volunteers asks me to dine
I thought it was much more than fine
I was even offered wine

I told them the truth
And they hired a sleuth
Who returned to me my youth
I am ready for a new dawn
I am no longer a pawn

King of the house

The mighty feline
Evolved over centuries
To hunt and prowl
And defend its territory
A vicious predator
Is now the royal leader in my home
I am his loyal subject
I bring him his caviar
In his personalised bowl
I let him steal my flesh
So he has a snack when I'm gone
I place a cushion on my knee
But his claws always stretch
For the treat that he loves
I hide in my quilt
But he sees it as play
Exploring the folds
like a new cave with every turn
I feel honoured to have
The king of Egypt with meow

The dilemma

In the beginning all was well
I had nothing much to tell
But then I entered hell

I had a job to do
But I then I had to poo
I could tell my friend did too

If I went first
And the toilet burst
I would forever be cursed

I tried to wait
I talked about a date
But I could not avoid my fate

I rushed to the bowl
the chicken took its toll
I wanted to hide in a hole

The smell that followed
Now that my gut had been hollowed
Oh how I wallowed

But my co-worker smiled
And made a joke like a child

I was forever exiled
We never reconciled

Poor partner

I sent my partner to drink
He threw up such stink
We are definitely out of sync
He says he's on the brink
That I'm missing a mental link
Wants to know if I'll re think
So I give him a knowing wink
That causes him to shrink
When I tell him my next kink

Bananas

Some bananas are pale,
Some bananas are dark
Some bananas have skin
While others have been peeled
Some bananas are soft
While others are just ripe
Some bananas are curved
A little to the right
Or a little to the left
While some are just the straightest
bananas that I have ever seen
Some bananas taste good
And some of them taste bad
But no bananas are my bananas
As the shop was all sold out

Tic Toc

Tic toc
The clock moves on,
One step closer to
deaths final knock
Tic toc
When the hands are broken
He still keeps time
He is the one
who has the key to your tomb
He knows from the moment you exist
When you'll take your final beat
Tic toc
That forgotten step
That misguided choice
That near miss
That slip in the ice
Tic toc
You come close every day
His arms are outstretched
Sometimes they pull
And sometimes they push
But they only grab once
Tic toc
You'll never be late
It's an appointment that everyone has
He's a guide for all

The short and the tall
The young and the old
Tic toc
Make the most of the days
Savour the hours
Drink in the minutes
And salivate on the fractions
You'll want them all when his finger extends

When the time comes

When the betrayal is flashed
And the rose tinted glasses have smashed
And the relationship has crashed
All plans have been dashed
And your heart has been slashed

There's nothing else for it
But to get emotionally fit
Climb out of the perilous pit
And find a way never to quit
You're more than this split

They say there's more fish in the sea
So don't go back with a plea
Even if he returns on bended knee
You were right in your choice to flee
You WILL find your great glee

The Silver Robin

The silver robin
Is more than myth
Residing in the ice,
The very depth of your depression
And just when you think
Your soul is frozen
From all the hurt
All the sorrow
All the injustice in the world
He is the flutter that
Beacons you back
He is the feeling
in the pit of your stomach
When you meet the one
When you get the job
That moment just before the kiss
He is the part of you
That stops you going cold forever
He brings forth the love
of those that have passed
And help you to stay up
When you want to stay down
His wings can light fire
That ignite the passion
You think you lost
When the darkness took over

He is the strength
From the depth of the earth
And length of the galaxy
He is you
And when you die
You send a warm feather
to everyone you love
So their robin
Will comfort them
With a little bit of you

The Longing

When you look beyond the window
And see the blowing leaves
Of gold and red
And some of green
And imagine, just for a moment
The feeling of floating free
Of leaving your cares
In your weary frame
And letting your spirit play.
To feel weightless
And yet comforted
By the refreshing ancient hug
To swirl high
And spiral low
To feel no pain
And feel no fear
Just for a moment
To linger in the life between the breaths
In a world inhabited by possibility
And hope
Where the worst has not yet happened
And might never happen still

www.ingramcontent.com/pod-product-compliance
Lightning Source LLC
LaVergne TN
LVHW010943200726
843509LV00013B/2276